Water Language

Water Language

Poems

PETER W. GORHAM

RESOURCE *Publications* • Eugene, Oregon

WATER LANGUAGE
Poems

Resource Publications
An Imprint of Wipf and Stock Publishers
199 W. 8th Ave., Suite 3
Eugene, OR 97401

www.wipfandstock.com

PAPERBACK ISBN: 978-1-7252-8898-0
HARDCOVER ISBN: 978-1-7252-8899-7
EBOOK ISBN: 978-1-7252-8900-0

12/21/20

Contents

O Lord Do I Lift Up My Soul

In my dream, the walls of my city have collapsed.
No psalms intone their way through the thick dust.
The city has collapsed. My soul is pinned down out there
Unbodied. Without it, I cannot easily
Unsieze my rusted parts but something persists me.
I sift through wreckage and dust, listening
For the faint moan. An acid mist rises and fires
My throat like the ovens.

When I find her, my arms and hands are heavy like driftwood.
Nothing can be lifted here. We wait and silently,
I try to comfort her, but my skin is barbed wire.
Only, in the evening, a quiet voice begins like leaves rustling
And the horizon draws in around us like a forest.

The scent of fir trees climbs and crosses itself
Undoing gently each star's clasp
In the sky. I can move my limbs again. We change
Together like the slow forest, over millennia.
We watch the Earth grow young beneath our feet
As we rise tandem above each orbit, above the comets.
It is my first birthday again, one candle shining like a star.

Triple Rainbow, *Hanalei* Bay

Our tongue is a mirror that tastes the rain
Our hands are a Stonehenge
Our eyes are a cipher that stands
Before any color can find
Its place in the sky's list.
Rain is our mother
Rain is our mother's mother
The Sun is our father
The Sun is our daughter
The sky is a place that is left
When we are gone.

If you say that we do not exist
Then we do not
And your eyes have become
A place that is left
A sky painted with the color blank
Stones at random on the edge
Of the land. If you say
That we do not exist
You are without a doubt
Correct, and the facts
Will never stray far from your feet.

(If you have seen us, then you know:
These facts can only speak their
Local dialect. Our speech is crisp
And as new as the dawn!
Listen as we unravel ourselves
For we are three words of a promise
That the heavens, balancing each day
Like a star on the crest of our seven shoulders
Have chosen never to forget!)

Arizona Memorial

Arizona of the fragrant mesquite, guarded
By the armies of the saguaro, and the blooms
Of the yucca plant, though sun and wind have ground
Your glass mountains into sand, I think each grain

Will become the seed of a new white pearl, and all
The water that has passed you by and filled
Some other country's skies, will rise
In every hollow where a lake has dreamed itself to be.

But your ship has gone down Arizona. And the oil
Does not stop rising. In the early morning
When the light has already begun to call down
The eastern stars, and the clouds begin to unravel

Off the tops of the *Ko'olaus*, it rises to the surface
And thins out in a silent pool of dying color
Until there is something too big for us
To ever remember.

I have thought I heard too many times the roar
Of approaching zeros, and (unlike you Arizona) slipped
My cables though the holding ground was good.
But when those north winds fill my sails and put

My rail down in a squall of too much blue freedom,
I turn again to harbors like yours,
Arizona, where time has pulled you into
Its iridescent shell, and the layers fold over you

And coalesce in a gentle caress
Where the oil grows clear
And seeps into the indigo, where the oil
Does not cease to rise.

Arizona of the fragrant mesquite, guarded
By the armies of the saguaro, and the blooms
Of the yucca plant, though sun and wind have ground
your glass mountains into sand, I think each grain

Will become the seed of a new white pearl, and all
The water that has passed you by and filled
Some other country's skies, will rise
In every hollow where a lake has dreamed itself to be.

A Code

All around me time whistles by
In a wind of small black needles.
My coffee stares back at me.
The echoes of old voices
Do not naturally diminish.
Music that I cannot quite make out
Follows me on the street as if for money.
Yet still

Sometimes I will stand like an old sycamore tree
At dawn, when the white mist
Settles on the world like gauze,
And the rivers have turned inward
To pay homage to the bones of their ancestors.
I listen for an ancient code,
Tapping itself out
On the inner edge of my body,
Tapping out
An unknown fortune,
In an alphabet that must be
A long way from its home.
I think it is the wild
Tahitian rhythm of silence itself
And if I could ever learn
The words to this song
Dancers will rise up around me like a forest.

Constellation

They seem too steep,
Too steep and too high:
These mountains, behind which
The stars grow
Their minerals, and cut
Their white crystal.

We are too deep in the mist,
Too deep to really see
Their clean cataracts of light.
But sometimes
When, for a moment,
A face that we had not recognized
As such, is suddenly clear and burns
Before us like a white hot blade

Then we can remember
The furnaces that forged
Our first thoughts from the coal fires.
Then we can remember the hammer
That shapes our bodies
Out of the ten-sided spaces,
And we can remember the sword
Of wisdom that is beaten out for us, quenched
And tempered in cool water like a baptism
Until its damask shines like living pearl.

Desert Rain

There is too much glory here.
In the wide part of this barren valley
The clouds have knit themselves
To the Earth with fire
And a gray curtain drawn
With nobody's permission. Already
The red-tailed hawk circling
Among the eastern foothills
Has seen the silver glint filling
The creek bed where she hunted
Yesterday, and she calls out
Her understanding to the wind.

This rain has fallen here before ten times
A thousand, and it has fallen
On the back of a green turtle
In the deep ocean, and it has waited
Ten thousand years in some Alaskan
Glacier, and it has fallen softly
In the face of someone we love. Yet
Today it will search out the face
Of the unloved desert, and smooth
The hardened brow, and be born again
Into the veins of the chaparral
Rising like strong wine to the high song
Of the midsummer stars.

Easter Dawn, Mt. Palomar, California

On the edge of a stand of small sequoias
Blue and shaggy still with darkness in
This last hour that the stars can still speak
In their high white voices, I wait while
Shadows fall like palm leaves from the eastern sky.

In this hour the sound of sirens will rake the cities
Fixing the newly dead into their final faces,
And a tomb will click shut like a padlock.
In this hour the tin cities stand grey and naked
Under the last stars, while the rivers of lead
Falter and pool in the sleeping suburbs.
No one is waiting for the sky
To possess them with a song of diamonds.

But here in these low mountains where the land
Has begun to rise and glisten, someone has
Unlocked the door of the east. Trees and grasses
Simmer like teapots in the low fire of the air.
Springs spill like liquor from the earth. The hands
Of the forests are full of aces, and the sky
Is wide and strung with bright opal.

Once in this same light, two women came first
To someplace where death had spent the last of its iron coins.
They found the locks were broken. They found death
Shot full of the arrows of God's peace.
They ran like children until their feet became
More beautiful than any dawn!

Extinction

It is a principle
Of something

That an animal
Is a kind of light

And that having
Come from a dusky

Place we cannot
Remember unable

Even to rekindle
Our own small fires

To a place
Of many candles

That we should not
Take it upon

Ourselves
To put
Them
Out

For Silence

The physicists say that silence itself
Spins with a sound too high for us to hear;
I am not convinced. I will tell you:
There is a rigging of quiet that tethers every moment
Cabling them down with the tension
Of unbearable fullness, full and absolute.

In the smooth gray of the fog that breasts
This California beach, empty and slick from
The hard fall of the afternoon tide, I learn again
That silence is a high language that the speech
Of the Earth can only imitate. That there is
Fragility more powerful than great strength.

That the cry of the unseen gulls can only
Pierce me this way if the hands of
Silence hold back what the gulls are not. That the surf
Empties its consonants upon the land
Each wave ending a single word of silence
That came before. I reach for it
But find it framed in nothing
That I can recognize.

But in a speech I have begun to understand
I have heard what the angel has said:
You have ears, now learn to hear!

Gale at dusk

When lightning fingers our horizon
And thunder marches its armored troops
Along our phosphorescent wake, the waves
Around us clap their hands, and sing
Their shanties in a wilder key.
Then the eyes of the jackal wind blink
And glitter in the gathering dark.

Such nights will fear come calling
Like a carpetbagger, planning only to
Rifle every white jewel of our joy. We wait
And let the Holy Spirit laugh him down
With a voice of sea and wind. This ocean
Plays rough with us, but we have come
Gladly to learn this game. We have traded
Our dusty faces and our five great
Career breaks for a white salt rime
And skin that turns to teak in the tropic sun.

Let it come:
Clouds that gather their robes like Sheiks
Clouds that harvest the sky like wheat
Clouds that frisk the sea like cops
Spindrift and wind steam, salt steam
Blue steam, the steam that circles the stars
That we cannot see. Steamroller hiss of everything else.

And the first drops of the deluge ring
Like silver coins on the deck: rain is
Our language, our currency; and our wealth
Will rise and break every bank
That keeps in chains this prisoned Earth.

Honolua Bay

We sail hard to the wind all afternoon while
Flying fish scatter like skipped stones
And a whale breaches far behind, crashing
The gold Sun's setting reverie. *Moloka'i* stands
Deep green in the haze of the west when we drop anchor
In the topaz calm of this hidden bay: *Honolua.*

Trade wind clouds swim over us
To a home in the blue shade, their
Eyes still watch the shepherd Sun.
The Moon sprinkles her tiny pearls
On their backs, soon she will
Cast our ship in her ancient silver.

Later, when she stands enthroned
Above us at the peak of the mast
We are changed: we are suspended
In glass. The sea floor questions us
With a face of smooth sand
How well do we know
The rhythm of our own name?

Honolua you are the one clean window
Into this house of God's water.
Your feet of crescent coral, your shoulders
Of green cliff, your mouth a blue
Stream laughing with brown *kukui* nuts
From the high forest rain; there is

No sleep, no hurt, no wound
So deep that it will make us forget
The arms of your solemn white surf
That baptized us into a body
That we thought we had lost.

'Iwa

As if an ancient and guttural language
Had translated itself into a silence of dark wings
And taken flight in the hollow space between
The newborn clouds. But something is lost:
Her soaring is a reprimand on our cities.
She rises, and the glass towers are unable
To look at her with their thousand eyes.

The city falls into sleep, and the *'Iwa*
Descends to her home in the barren island.
She hears again below her the surf
Sacking the riches of the crescent beach
She sees again above her the Moon
And greets it by a name she only knows
She folds again her wings around her like a poem.

Alexander and Boukephalos

This prince knows the color of things
That burn on the inside.
Boukephalos, coal black
Under the sweat that flecks him
Remembers this red maze
Of men's faces around him
From the battle charge, but here
He is caught in a thicket of leather strap.
He waits in his madness
For the spear thrust
But his heart feels only
The stab of the trader's taunt.

Yet now his eye finds something
Clear and golden among
The black beards and glare
Of the market square.
Suddenly there is nothing else.
He finds he has become
A young foal again, all legs.
This prince comes near
His blonde fire cools
The raging in Boukephalos.
And Alexander, mounting him
In the center of a huge

Silence that begins to range out
Across the Earth like bright
Circles in a dim pond
Astounds them all except himself.

Erebus and *Terror*: Ross Island, Antarctica

Two-headed white dragon crouched in the far white ice
As if it could hide you like the savannah
But your simmer and smoke tell us the tale. Beauties
You are, though. I want to lose myself in your glistening
Blue glacier falls that drink in every drop of sky light
Grinding off slowly every hard muscle of the rock beneath.
Twenty white-hard miles stand between us
Two hundred white-frosted crevasses offering
Quick passage to the underworld. Strong men
Have you seen who left their bodies there.

Two giants did you also watch, craving the glory
Of the utter South, Scott and Shackleton, no taller
Than other men, but their spirits rose like monoliths.
One returned, finding that the lives of his men were
Brighter lights than any glory in that white hell;
One did not. For Captain Scott, Ross Island hid her face
At the bitter cold end, and felled them short by a day or two.
We cannot fault him for his magnificence.

Perhaps you saw him, tall *Erebus*,
When you lifted up your head: the third man,
Who sailed by your island for another route, thinking like
The Norseman that he was. Sly and cunning student
Of all of Winter's weapons, all her strategies, her weakness
For a hundred good Greenland dogs. Amundsen made

Quick work of those armies of glaciers, leaving Scott,
Five weeks behind him, a tent and flag of Norway on the spot,
A wound he and his friends would not survive.

Shackleton will I always love, like a father he
Cherished his men and would not give them up
For the last hundred mile prize, not leave them
Rotting shipwrecked on a frozen island.

Scott I will revere, for his English oaken spirit
His arctic tractor, his brave ponies, holding
Fast to his duty and character to the last, scrawling
The last few beats of his heart into words forever full of power.

But Amundsen will I try to imitate, not because
His wisdom was more full of romance or beauty
Than his peers—and it was not. Not because I am more ready
To admire him, who planned to eat his dogs, and did so
Without remorse on the journey back.

Rather, he honored what was true about the place
And what was not. It was the mark of
Ice-hard scarred leather in his soul, won
By sparring with his romance until he stabbed it
Through the heart.

Times there are
That God will rescue those not yet
Equipped for their fate
And times there are
That He will not.

Kiawe **on** *Moloka'i*

The *kiawe* tree the brush the *kiawe* wood
Has crowned this country better than
A forest could. Someone has laid
Their fences far around this land
And kept us out.

Hoping this morning to gain the beach
Three miles up around
The broken lava point called *Ilio*,
We have to laugh, not being
Out of our bodies yet.
There is no bloodless parting of this
Kind of sea. Only: a shade of leaf

Green like olivine, an aroma
That pools around us in the lull
Of the wind, so that we sometimes
Mistake it for color.
And thorns that need no testing
Of their thorn-worthiness.

It is a strange wilderness this
Myriad acres of thorn empire
Without any keeper of the club's
Agenda, or waiting list for the winnebagos.
And something there is about a beach
That you find you cannot reach.

Thorns, you sober me down, but still
I am drawn to your view of the world,
The one you make no effort here to hide.
If one man's brow did once in
Perfect silence turn you into crown
Then I will take your green as gold
And go my way.

King Solomon's Wings

I have sent my mistral dreams
Across the hieroglyphic sea
I have interviewed the heavens
With astronomy
I have spent a paper treasure
On what I knew it could not buy
And after all I find that wisdom
Still calls after me, she calls to me.

When gold can buy me nothing golden
Other than itself; when diamonds
Are as common as a block of coal
When *Eros*, grown old, no longer
Darts a pang inside my soul,
Then silence, closing its canopy
Around me while the fingers of
Evening touch my throat

Surrenders its army to one cricket
Who mines for something hidden
In the tone of the dusk.
I think: why has not God
Made these cricket's wings
To fly, as fishes' fins
Are made to swim?

But Wisdom says:
God made these wings
To sing to Him.

Mānoa Stream

Overhead the leaves
Woven green mirrors
Reflect the rain

The water a voice
That no longer
Speaks our name

Highwater mark
Hiplevel two days ago
Shoal reach with taro
And shreds of old
Cardboard not yet
Unrecognizable

Mānoa stream
Why do your secret
Songs no longer
Include us?

What god has
Withdrawn into the arms
Of your twining banyans?

Swimming in Sea Caves, *Kona* Coast

The rain comes sleepwalking slowly down
From the coffee groves twelve hundred feet
And four miles up the shoulders of this young
Volcano. We stand on the rim of the western shore
Where red *pahoehoe* once boiled these placid
Blue pools and bombed its way into the surf
Until it took the shape of a clear basin:
Kealakekua.

Past the south end, where the beach withdraws itself
And the *hale koa* rises up to hide it well
We dive and play like young otters in a small cove
Graced by a smooth dark lava wharf, uncarved by
Anyone. A single ancient iron cleat
Sheds its snakeskin rust on the black rock
To which it is bolted, the last memory of
Ships and men whose names once harbored there.

Swimming down, we find an open cave below
Green light shimmering from the far and unseen end.
We breathe in deep, swim down and inward, where six of us
Could easily go abreast. The bright circle ahead grows
And churches us finally in a silver pool, rock roofed and full
Of strange whispers that call from each hollow to another

Passing on messages that we cannot decode.
They hesitate, as if they noticed us, and then
They surge again, remembering the slow drum
Of the sea outside which will not let them rest.

Five pools we find along this luminous trail through
A lava tube. Five uncut jewels that ran with the red fire
Once. The first people of this island learned
The signs of the water's voice and all the facets
Of the blue light. They knew which syllables
Could pacify their deities, which names were never
Meant to be spoken.

In this same bay, the centuries have rarified his name,
Lono our captain, our navigator, and sometimes
Our god. James Cook, he was born, but here
Peacemaker, and warmaker, he passed on from this world,
Slaughtered by priests.

It is not the first time that a people pondering the gift
Of their God's presence in the flesh
Have found such fortune hard for them to bear.

Mermaid Song

O when I lived in the green weed forests
At the bottom of the sea, and spoke every morning
To an old coelacanth on the slopes of a red volcano,
Each day my spirit drifted like a secret
Fragrance in the hills of the blue wilderness.

Then a spark came up from the center of the Earth
And spun its clean arms like a galaxy
Calling out the colors of the invisible sky:
O sky of water
O stars of phosphorescence,
O clouds of flashing fish that polish
All the edges of the Sun
O sands that hide the halibut. . .

But one day I lifted up my head above the waves
And felt the wind that brushed me with its golden hair
It spoke of islands and carried some in its pocket
It spoke of the seven continents standing
On the shoulders of old volcanoes
It spoke of the cities, and imitated for me
The sound of their million flags beating endlessly.

Now those hungry cities spread their nets for me
And bury the waves in their bureaucracy.
They scrape away the blue frescoes from the dome of the sky.
All that enter them soon fall into their given appointments.

But a spark has arisen in me from the bottom of the sea
And spun its lightning arms like a new galaxy
Calling out the names of the unseen sky:
O sky of water
O stars of phosphorescence,
O clouds of flashing fish that polish
All the edges of the Sun
O sands that hide the halibut. . .

Moonstone

I find it in a dry riverbed
I grasp it in the hollow of my hand
I have forgotten my hand
I have forgotten the riverbed.

You are the white moonstone in my hand.
Its light is your light
Its round face is your face
Its smooth face is the bright
End of many winters.

One day my mouth
Dries up. It has become that forgotten
Riverbed. My tongue has the taste
Of sand. It has the taste
Of ashes.

The night sky becomes a negative:
Stars shine like black quartz against
A blinding white anything.
I have lost the white stone
I have lost my name
My hand is too hollow.

New Growth on the Edge of an LA Sidewalk

Little palm, risen from a pavement crack
I have seen your green bundle sparrowing
In the shadows of the concrete arroyo.
No one makes you do this. Child of a dry
And broken seed, fallen in among the dust
Of the city's bones, you have chosen not
To be nothing, yet you are born
Already numbered on the ticking lists.

Tomorrow they may pull you up, but tonight
In an hour of silence when your leaves fold up
Like small hands, your color flashes quietly
Through my citygray dreams until I remember

That somewhere a wave is rising to the stars
Unhindered, up between the drifting continents,
Answering for every island that no longer has a voice.
That somewhere a white arch stands
Under which I will one day also
Walk out of myself.

A Conversation with the Sky

Sky you have fallen into my friend's eyes
And then you looked away.

Blue is the color of reflection, and light
Must follow such laws as know it.

Sky, you have staked around me
My own solitude like a tent
And covered the mountains
With your cloudy draperies.

Only in solitude can you comfort
The loneliness of God.

But even among the rivering crowds
You drift above me like something unsaid
A word without vowels.

What I am
Is written again
Each day for you.

Unlimit yourself
And your day will be all days
Written with the blue scribe
Among the hidden stars.

Curvature

When we became clever the Earth shrank itself
Into the head of a pin, surrounded by angels
Its curvature now a real number with infinite digits.

There are rivers in the skies, and swept down one of them
I find myself far from you, months away but only hours away.
How can we really learn what space is, its viscosity,
When the heat is always set to a boil? At midnight
The Moon stands upended, its light arriving in a heartbeat.

If only my life could bend more easily than the space I am in.
Instead the clay jar around my scroll
Fractures easily. My words dry up and fragment
Dispersing like flakes of ash into the white noise.

But a music of meaning still stands unbodied somewhere;
Well-tempered, no ratios of numbers will capture it today.
Lacking words, but curving around the Word itself,
The Reason, the *Logos*, the one and clearest ringing note no
Bell can yet attain. When it rings
Our bones will gather again
And body themselves into an army.

November Lines

For the unexpected eclipse, when the Moon
Gathers us for a moment under her satin cloak
For love, when we finally learn her winter night name
For silence, and its unmarked wells in the desert
For no place that we can imagine.

For the empty dream rivers
Which our hearts long to fill
With a new water symphony,
Music that must always exceed us

(Have the trees not already
Unbound their leaves, now they are
Christened with stars' blood?
Has the ice not already somewhere
Trimmed the ponds in its thin silk?
Is there nowhere already a vow
Made that will never be broken?)

On Finding Indian Grindstones in the Forest

Mt. Palomar, California

I walk in the borrowed shade of oaks, and listen
To leaves that shift together like shoals of green fish
In the wind. Do these trees and their cedar cousins still
Remember the people that printed their lives
On these strange tables of rock, to which
This forest moors itself against the rising tide
Of cities from the south and west?

These people were no industrious Incas
Peppering their landscape with pyramids
And inventing civilization before
They had invented gunpowder. Acorns
And deer they found in these woods; water
And stone; wind rising through the trees
With the sound of an invisible ocean;
The rhythm of woodpeckers and their
Redheaded children. It is no mystery
That the holes in these stones are so deep.

Here, thirty yards up from the small spring,
Is the oldest of these Indian cornerstones.
The hands of women whose names have passed
Out of any living speech ground their acorns
Deeper into these basins until they found the bottom

Of this foot-thick table of old granite. One year
They returned from their winter home to find
A small cedar had risen from a stray seed
Fallen through the bottom of their oldest rock
And, emerging slowly until it could not be restrained,
Split it down the center.

Only the stump remains now.
One hundred thirty-five rings I count
Under the saw marks that have taken
This tree since. My eyes rest finally on
The center: heartwood that unfolded its own
Small whisper to the ears of those who would not
Cut it down for newsprint or lead pencils.

As the grey light glides off somewhere to the west
This book of leaf and rock that God
Has bound together in this mountain grove
Without words, but leaves of oak and ash
And dreams colliding softly like the clouds,
Opens, slowly, and imperceptibly
Begins another verse.

On the Beach at Los Gatos

On the beach at Los Gatos
Under a sky full of broken worlds
I pull myself down deep into
The warm hollow of my bones
And dream:

I am a Leatherback sea turtle.
My eggs are laid and covered.
The sea is returning. The salt grass
Is hissing quietly in the wind.

The Moon, sharp crescent, draws sparks
From the facets of my back.
The first wave of the new tide rises around
My body like warm silver.

Something else can now begin.
This is the wind
That I must breathe
This is the sea
That I must swim.

A Dirge for Two Children, Fallen Through Ice

In the dusk, the empty aspen trees
Stand like white knives in the parks.
Shadows spill from every street. The fall
Of the blue night snow muffles the small bells
Of the rivers. If we were fish, we could give up,

Sink into our own thick blood, go slow, and save
Our nickel skins until the flash of green Spring.
Twelve trout in twenty minutes I have caught
Thinking that way, or perhaps, in the cold vise
Not thinking at all.

O Children, your bodies can never remember
What it was to be a fish. They are strange metal,
Annealing themselves in the deep ice bellies of the lakes.
How wonderful you must have seemed to them!
Breaking through the roof of heaven
With a great crack and a shout; yet it was

A baptism that we never asked of you.
O Children, if God has taken you to be
Two Suns in the starry crown of the north
Then who will thaw the gray silence
That frosts the windows of our towns?

(In the east, the clouds are torn, and the stars
Drop like pearls from a broken strand of sky.)

Galleon

Three months out from Manila
Scurvy creeping on aboard like poison fog
Prayers and rosaries worn down among salt-dried fingertips
One sailor's childhood wounds resurge
And bleed ragged like new again. There will be more.
A storm, boiling down from the undiscovered Alaskan
Gulf, frays every will's fiber until the strands are torn
And hope curls into a fetal ball. What porcelain, what spice,
What silk is worth those bodies sliding into the deep
Sewn into sailcloth, but now perhaps
Finding some kind of peace in the cool silence there.

One day those gray false lines of landscape turn true
Punta Concepción rises dreamlike in the east.
Revived, those sailors still able to climb their rig
Are up in a moment and hope lifts every breast.
The coast is less a haven than a wall to guide
The wind and waves, and turning south
The ship, grown heavy of weeds and shell beneath
Still finds her steady way. New to the route
The captain stands in close when the light is good
But lifts her clear of danger to the west at night.

With five weeks of coastal rhythm, Acapulco begins
To seem possible again. Endless northwest winds and current
Have warmed their blood and bodies until the world seems
Gentle in its turning. But one day, as evening draws in
A blue haze to the east, the sailors are silent, ill at ease.
A gray line stands far off the starboard bow
Where nothing should be. They bear off to the west,
Climbing as high as the beaten sails and foul bottom
Will allow. It will not be enough. *Bahia Vizcaino*
That ancient bay of whales and shoals, curls its eddies
Around them, slow and somber in the last embrace.

Embayed: in the sailors' ancient tongue, *empeñado*. Their lives
Pawned away in the deep crescent of that bay, driven gently
But firmly, wearing back and forth, by morning all souls
Aboard now know the voyage will soon end.
Fear fingers its way under each one's ribs, finding the space
It will choose when the time is come. In the distance
There is something white, a low murmur, rising slowly.
When it comes, the surf holds back a bit, and she settles
Stern-to on a shoal, pounding with each swell,
But still not broken yet. By evening those who can
Will gather in the deepening chill of the windswept beach.

A fire, burning sodium-yellow from the driftwood there
Keeps the coyotes off, and gives some warmth
Displacing for a moment the darkening dread.
A desert of sand and wind, dunes and lagoons,
In this kingdom of salt, death is patient and will wait
A few more days or weeks. It will not be that long.
Already a runner for the local *Cochimí* tribe
Has signaled his chief to the enemy camp.
Young men, thirsting to prove their warrior hearts
Leap like cheetahs down trails they made

For this shining moment in their lives. Death
Has many friends in this salt wilderness.

Four centuries later, that beach still strands the lost
Bleached white bones of a dozen whales, and the roughened
Ribs of wood and steel from unremembered ships.

And for the sharpest eyes, the stunning glint of blue and white
From bright *Ming* shards, five-clawed dragons severed
By the crash of ballast stones they rode into the surf.
In pieces they remain
Imperial, quiet guardians in this holy place.
Wan Li and his court, and those who sailed
In hope of capturing that grace
Are not forgotten here.

Peregrine Falcon

Rising in long arcs along thermals
From the floor of the saguaro-studded
Desert five miles down and out to the southwest
You become the unspoken answer to everything
A name which is not going to be repeated.

Once, wheeling slowly around the hips
And hollows of the manzanita ridges
Above me, you stop, fixing a place
Between two halves of the air; between
Two pulses of the blood, the inside
And the outside. Only your eyes can still
Remember the Earth.

And in the last red of the dusk
I catch sight of you again, shaping
A cool unmoving darkness against
The returning night sky. Gold Arcturus
Appears along the curve of your wingtip.

I do not see you finally
Turn and drift off
But already you have defined
A new geometry: your eye
A star, your body
An unheard of
Constellation.

Riding at Anchor: *Kaneohe* Bay

(Two miles southwest of the Marine Corps Air Station)

The Moon spreads her moss of light
Deep across the sleeping countries to the east
But here she roosts for a while
On the watery edge of the world.
In a moment the blue silence is knifed dead
By jet engines roaring in their power lust
Fierce lions we have bound to our country's cause.
Tonight good and evil are drinking together at
The local pub, and Marines are practicing.

Words on paper blow like scattered chaff amid this
Hurricane falsetto howl, which will
Almost surely shatter every wineglass
That we hoped might still be spared. They
Will have their fire feast it seems. Only
Let me have this calm cove tonight.
Let my two palms touch together again
The Moon's white web.

Anchor chain grates on some deep coral head
Like distant cannons. The snapping shrimp
Still crackle in their prosperous homes
Of the night. Small waves sing gracefully
Along the hull their own magic libretto.
Too soon sleep folds me like a paper doll

Just as the shore flowers send out their
Lovely promises, brushing across my face like
Airy spindrift in this dream's gale.

Self Portrait in Fractals

You have thought that times have lengths
That moments are spliced like sinnet
Fathom by fathom down into the seasons.
A hurricane has invented you
But you boxed it up with geography
And put it in a new catalogue of winning surfaces.

Between what can never stop, and what has yet
To begin. Between the edge of nothing
That you cannot yet name. I am talking
About the boundaries, I am talking about
The thin lights, I am talking because
Of what I cannot contain, because
I cannot contain myself. I am
Not going to be able to finish
What I have never begun.

Song for Night

A thousand stars
Were foundries for
The living cinder
That we are tonight

Night has its cauteries
Which will fuse
What can be fused;
Night has its boundaries.

Night has its seas
In which all deeps begin
Night has its skies
In which all heights will end.

The Moon Part

It is the time of the white plume and dragons
Have proliferated in the oceans. The blue-edged
Tools of the wise cry out in their disuse. Cities
Blister in the sore places of the Earth
And the mountains shift their feet
Impatiently, waiting for the end.

But we will wait next to
The cool cistern of our bodies until
Heaven's rain shouts its water language
Over all our horizons and every word becomes
A tributary to a new and unknown ocean.

We will then take our ships
To the Moon part of this ocean where
The Moon never turns her face
From the window because
She can still see herself
In the mirrors of the Earth.

Song for the Sea God

Your surf plays lightly on the white keys
Only, Poseidon, when you dream of us
In your deep coral bed. When you rise
The seas shake out their great manes, and toss
Their heads to the sky. Their blue herds
Graze endlessly around the world, visiting
Every clean field of the nine winds.
Their white stallions cradle bright planets
In their wings, and there are no numbers
For the earthquakes that will follow them.
But still you sleep, O white-haired one.
Your diligent waves practice carefully
The same andante.

O Man of the ocean, even time
Will drag its anchors when your slumber ends.
Send your sea wind up among the dead ribs
Of this city; let your waves raid the lobbies
Of a hundred skyscrapers, and your tides carve
Their sea caves in a thousand city blocks!
Let your green islands ring out like bells
Until their music falls like clear rain
On our sandpaper shoulders;
Let them storm us with their wild guitars
Until they turn our nut-brown voices
Into sapphires!

The Albatross

Because my solitude is richer and more ancient than
All dynasties, you are welcome
To share my wealth of salt wind and wave.
Your spirit has wings that you have never tried.
Dip and soar then, not letting
Your wingtip ever quite
Touch the sea. Search out these
Latitudes where ice and ocean
Know each other by a hundred names.

And if, one morning, in the gray chalklight
Of a Southern ocean dawn, when the seas
Send their banners of spray down the torrents
Of the blind wind, you find suddenly
That you are alone, and that everything
Has gathered itself into one voice
Which chooses not to speak, then you have become
My companion, and our two skies
Will always find each other again in their season.

Because my body is a white cross spanning
Every sentence of the Southern ocean sun
Because my heart is an arrow nocked
Into the taut bowstring of the wind
Because to see me here is to begin
To know me other than the stars
And storms in which I choose to live.

The First Voyage

The first voyage begins in the far lee
Of a forgotten summer, where the windrose
Falls in on itself, and the blue sargasso
Lanes begin to widen and disperse. Here
You find yourself expand and simplify

Your shadow falling from you in arcs
Of blue splinters. But there is nothing
To recover. There is no longer any light
Which you cannot begin to reflect, or any line
Which does not radiate from you or through you.

Take this chart and plot the one true line
Which you can draw into yourself, to mingle
With your bloodline, and draw it
Singing wire tight, across the unspeakable.

The Leaf People

When they speak their voices glint
For a moment like nickles
Among the leaf noise
But they are soon lost
In the infinite rustle.

Their breath is woodshade
Their food lies down among
The roots of things which
Only their feet can know.
At times they imagine their

Knees will multiple like cattle
And clasp. With their arms
The may imitate trees, but
No bird flickers there.
Alongside them no creeks can glitter.

When they die they sift
Down among the leaves
And sleep, and their dreams
Rise up like mute
Pilgrims in the morning mist.

The Ocean is a Fire

The ocean is a fire
That burns because it is made
Of what it cannot quench.
Green flame, blue flame, and the blue coals
That burn their phosphor nightly
Like paper lanterns in the deep.

The ocean is a fire
With waves of flame that sweep clean
The coalescing foam of the romantic flair
It burns in a storm of silence
It burns in a silence of unwritten storms
It tears up the scripts and burns them one by one.

But I'll swear no fire would I rather watch
Licking the world with its great cat tongue
No fire would I care to watch that could not
Burn from me in a moment every unclean
Gestapo thought that jams me on all my stations
No fire that did not whisper to the fluid that I am.

The ocean is a fire
That burns because it is made
Of what it cannot quench.
Green flame, blue flame, and the blue coals
That burn their phosphor nightly
Like paper lanterns in the deep.

Columbus and the Arawaks

> They have no iron. . .with 50 men
> I could subjugate them all.
>
> —Columbus' Diary

Columbus, his hauberk shining in the dawn light
While his ships fill the harbors of the new world
Like stadiums, stands tall among the
Wide-eyed Arawaks. Gifts they bring him:
Balls of cotton, and parrots green
As emeralds.

Columbus sees the green
And dreams of emeralds. He sees the Sun
Rising golden in the east, and dreams
Of gold. But Columbus sees no gold among
The gifts of the Arawaks. He dreams
They have stolen his dream.

Enslaved on their own land, their children
Killed and maimed for entertainment
The desperate Arawaks begin to leave
Their own bodies, having no other answer to
The steel that laughs at their cane
Hunting spears.

But Columbus, rising like
A saint over the horizons of Europe,
Eclipses these shadow things with the glint
Of Arawak gold, and few hundred lucky
Arawak slaves, his entourage. By 1540 they were gone
None left where once a quarter-million lived.

Columbus if we have become
Your wide-eyed dream of gold and
Silicon and gasoline and boobjobs and
The damp growth of dollars in which we
Revel and graze, then let us someday
Awake to serve as the glad slaves
Of the gentle spirits of the Arawaks.

And God if you can find still find
The green shoot of mercy
That your man Columbus left unwatered, then
Forgive him Lord, because he was no worse
Or better than other men
And sometimes even knew it.

Three Stones

To see what shape is pressed
Into the palms of earth that hold them
I turn them out, and find no mark that I can know.
Their pockets fill with rain and fragments of the sinking Moon
Shipwrecked among the clouds in the western sky.
Three stones that wait for nothing in the dark
Three pools that pull the sky into the Earth
Three candles that the Moon and summer rain have set
Like a cipher at my feet.

Lord these voiceless stones speak louder than light
Of the streams that you have sent
To shape them, but I am still a stone of flesh
All edge, and fumarole from which
Sound spalls like flakes of new sulfur.

Stone and water, and the colors that begin with them
Will always repeat themselves in this light
Until something rises in the shadows from behind them
And flies, quicker than any hawk
And takes the Moon like a white wafer in its beak.

The Dolphins

It is afternoon when they arrive. Under sail:
Main and genoa, as we follow the chalkline
Contrails in the sky to Honolulu, back to
Who we were two weeks ago

The Plan, the many numbers
That prick our fingertips, the doors
The have stolen our names.
Duty, that old brown buzzard
Wheels patiently above us at a safe height.
His sharp eyes have not forgotten us.

These dolphins do not swim with us for the gifts
We can give them; we have none.
All things are their gifts.
All days are their birthdays.
How can there be anything that they do not want?

While they surf in our bow wave
We reach down our hands to cross
Into their continent, but they move shyly
Out of reach. Yet we drink each others' eyes
With an undivided thirst, and our voices
Navigate with vowels in a sea without language.
They do not swim with us because they need us.

They have peopled these deep countries
Without war; they have peopled our silence
With their inscrutable speech. Their joy
Burns in us like a soft fire
As the last of them, steel grey and young
With eyes shining like silver dimes, turns finally
Back to the wide blue forest of his home.

To a Friend I Have Wronged

How easy it is to count those
Pillar-of-salt choices that put me here
At the wrong end of this empty telescope
Wishing I was nobody, but unable to
Shake the white sore that is my name.

And when I am done counting them
My spirit is bankrupt. My heart
Is a self-inflicted wound. My feet
Have taken root in a waterless country.
My voice cracks like black shale.

My friend, now you have seen what the dark glass
Can do to a face that you loved
How the silt can choke up
Any clear river that watered and softened
The boundaries between our lives.

What my words have charred will crumble into dust
But there is a better fire out of which all glass
Will rise up clean and pure
There is a river where all the silt
Falls to the deep and returns to the fertile Earth
There is one man, our eldest brother

Whose name is the fire, whose name is the river
Who holds the sword and the golden book
And calls the nine planets by their hidden names
When we pile our tenpenny coals at his feet
His love for us will burn them into diamonds.

Manu O Kū

Fairy Tern

A grove of *kukui* nut trees
Is all it takes
To change the world forever.
White feather fairies
Inhabiting the flash of tropic
Snow among the greens
Crush me with a weight
Of wonder that lifts even
The heaviest of the dull aches here.

Paired for life
They cleave apart the blue
Like two white razors
Two-part inventions of
The God we barely know

And there they go
Again, wheeling and diving
Like two hands
Signing to the heavens
explaining what
No words will ever do
Manu O Kū

Whale Song

The wind has fallen asleep with the Sun
And the Moon has found another window
For the night. The sea beneath us breathes
In a gentle rhythm, and we lay becalmed
Honored guests in this solemn congress of stars
That meets around us to choose the colors of the sky.

Three times a minute, or so, a meteor
Flashes like a blue sword from Perseus.
In the black water below new stars are born
With a blue-green flash of phosphorus.

An island, two miles to the north of us,
Shadows us carefully, and now and then
Captures a star with its dark arms.
Incense of flowers hangs like forgiveness in the air.

And in the deep hours, when the tired eyes
Of the small towns have fallen dim
And the flames of the stars' candles stand up
Like clear angels, then we hear a song
Rise around us from the unreachable canyons
Of water over which we drift.

It is the song of souls that have been inlaid
With uncountable centuries of innocence
It is the clean song of those who will not
Remember the uncountable wrongs we have done them.

We sit humbly in the last pew of this chapel
And let the wild beauty of these psalms
Splinter our significance. These simple friars
Whose friends are the stars and
Whose friends are the white albatrosses
Have remembered to pray for us tonight.

Window Seat over the High Sierra

I am halfway
To the airless place that
Marks the edge of the first heaven
Where the Sun's hands endlessly
Brush the sky's blue coat
Until it always faintly glows.
And I am in love
With the Earth again.

O Earth for all
Those black nights these flying things
Took me to a place
I did not want to be
This one bright window awaited me
Like a love letter.

O Earth, and your thousand mountains
I love your wrists of speckled ice!
With your knees in the
Morning snow, and your little
Ice lakes in their silver
Pouches on your belt
You haven't seen me yet
Though my eyes are bigger than planets!

Washington

I am standing at the base of your monument
On the clearest of sapphire blue mornings
With the warm sun at my back I press up close
And lift my gaze along the spire above

It rises into the heavens like a stone road
Smoother than any that lay before you
In those warring wasteland years that beggared you
Before faithless Congress who never could
Fathom the depth of your inner democracy.

O Father, when you had sunk into the mire
Of frozen hell in Valley Forge, how did you
Restrain your righteous hand against my forefathers

My brothers, who would not sell you grain, hiding it
Instead for their double-down on the British? You had
Every right to fire our barns down to dust, but
You forgave our mud-faced lies, our greed, our littleness.

Standing now far above us at the highest heaven end
Of that gleaming stone blade, you have watched
Your revolution become a monument, a history,
A vision of hunger that land and wealth alone will

Never abate. When you laid down your gleaming sword
At Congress' feet, when you gave up your throne
For a farmer's rake, when you laid down the world
Gently, lowering it from your Atlas shoulders
We should have seen your skyward vision
And memorized it in a better way
Than stone monuments.

Tekhenu, Sky-piercer,
When will we see you again,
Tall and full of grace
Riding in the distance,
just rounding the far bend
On the trail ahead, half-hidden
In the Appalachian mist?

Hope

Today I cannot look myself in the eye.
The tall pines that stood for me
And set their lovely shade around my heart
Have all been massacred by the machine.
Those straight masts and moonwhite sails
That rose up like promises yesterday over the horizon
Have since changed course and carried
Their cargo to another port. My body still
Flourishes like a mountain stream in the spring melt,
But my spirit feels the first early winter frost.

I wish I were that great cross of wings, the albatross
That my body dreams itself to be. I wish
That something would bloom in the night
Taking its form slowly and carefully
In the cool of the darkest hours, dividing itself
From the emptiness, drawing up from the Earth
A new name and a clear voice, and become a prayer
So that God would see it and lean to catch
Its fragrance, in the first hour of a morning
Glistening with fresh dew. I wish I were
A country-strung garland, to crown and guard
The center of my body's door forever.

Notes

Throughout the work I have tried to be consistent in the use of the *'Okina*, or glottal stop, which is an important part of the transliterated Hawaiian language, appearing sometimes even before the first vowel of a word. I have indicated Hawaiian words with italics througout. Some other proper names are also italicized where it seemed appropriate.

"Triple Rainbow, *Hanalei* Bay." The title refers to the combination of the primary, secondary, and tertiary bow, the latter of which appears just to the inside of the primary bow, with color order reversed compared to the primary. These are not uncommonly seen in Hawaii, but are rare elsewhere.

"Arizona Memorial" takes its title primarily from the USS Arizona, sunk in World War II, the wreck of which is now a part of the Pearl Harbor National Memorial.

Honolua Bay is at the northwest end of the island of Maui.

The *'Iwa* is known also as the Great Frigate bird outside of Hawaii. They are visible from great distances, soaring with a wingspan of 7–8 feet.

"*Erebus* and *Terror*: Ross Island, Antarctica." The title refers to the two largest mountains on the icebound Ross Island, which were named for the two ships of James Clark Ross' expedition to Antarctica c. 1840. Mt. Erebus, the larger of the two, is an active volcano over 12,000 feet in elevation, dominating the view from the Ross Island scientific research stations of the U.S. and New Zealand.

Kiawe is the name given in *Hawai'i* to several species of mesquite bushes and trees native to South America, introduced in *Hawai'i* in the early 19th century. It is now endangered in its native habitat, but very widespread in Western *Moloka'i* on other parts of the islands. Thorns can be up to 4 inches long in some varieties.

"Swimming in Sea Caves, *Kona* Coast." *Kealakekua* Bay on *Hawai'i* Island (known by most as the Big Island) was the home to a large population of native people at the time Capt. James Cook first arrived. It was a religious and cultural center as well. Due to a coincidence of his arrival with a local prophecy, it appears that he was deified by the local priests as the god *Lono*, which likely later led to his death. There is a monument to the event at the head of the bay, accessible only by boat or a rather steep trail.

"On Finding Indian Grindstones in the Forest." The relic bedrock mortars and metates are on the property of the Palomar Observatory at the summit of Mt. Palomar, where the author performed astronomical research. The Indians of the area were named by Spanish settlers the *Luiseños;* their native name is unknown, but they belong linguistically to the Shoshonean family, and had likely occupied the area for many centuries before the Spanish arrived.

"Galleon," takes its title from the Manila Galleons, a class of ship used in the Spanish-Asian trade during the 15th and 16th centuries. Ming dynasty China did not allow foreign ships to enter their ports, so the trade was conducted in the Phillipines. The trade was so lucrative that even the large number of shipwrecks did not diminish the Spanish investment in these voyages. The author participated in a search for one of these ships, which was eventually located, in Bahia Vizcaino, the "heel" of the boot of Baja California.

"Riding at Anchor: *Kaneohe* Bay." Marine Corps Base *Hawai'i* is a U.S. Marine Corps facility and air station located on the *Mokapu* peninsula which partially encloses *Kaneohe* Bay, a large, originally pristine coral-bound bay on the eastern coast of *O'ahu*.

"Manu O Kū" takes its title from the Hawaiian name for the White Fairy Tern, or White Tern, a small seabird of the *Laridae* family, commonly found nesting in *Kukui* trees in *Hawai'i*. Their chicks hatch from an egg balanced on a branch with no nest, born with grey coloring that match the branches they spend their early lives on. At maturity they become a very pure white. They are excellent and acrobatic flyers, foraging for fish far off the coast during the day, and returing with a fish in their beaks in the early evening for their chicks.

"Whale Song." Humpback whales visit the Hawaiian islands in great numbers during the winter, migrating from the North Pacific to breed and bear calves. Their other-worldy songs carry great distances beneath the surface, and are especially common to hear, coupling well to the hull of a boat, in the shallower waters between *Moloka'i, Maui*, and *Lana'i*.

Acknowledgements

"On the beach at Los Gatos," was published in early form in a student publication at the University of *Hawai'i* at Mānoa, but the publication is no longer extant and the details of publication name and date are lost.

"For Silence" was published in an early form by a journal called *The Other Side*. The journal is no longer extant, and the details of publication date are lost.